Faith Is Like Chocolate

To Anaiah
Love Darla

Darla Noble

Stay true to God!

To my Gasconade Christian Service Camp 'family'—you have blessed my life in countless ways and I thank God every day for each and every one of you.

Faith Is Like Chocolate

You probably don't remember the first time you tasted chocolate, do you? The first piece of chocolate to touch your lips probably came from your grandma, your Sunday school teacher or the nice lady at the bank.

Where you got it isn't really all that important, though. Why you ate it...that's what matters.

Think about it...chocolate isn't the prettiest thing to look at. It's a little slab of brown stuff with lines and words on it, or a small cylinder-shaped piece of brown goo (aka the Tootsie Roll®).

You know, when you actually take the time to stop to think about it, chocolate doesn't look very appetizing, does it?

So why did you eat it? You ate it because you trusted the person who gave it to you. When they told you how good it would be, you believed them.

But what happened after that? What happened after you took that first bite? You *did* take another bite, didn't you?

Of course you did! The question, though, is why? Why did you take the next bite...and the next (and the countless ones after that)?

You kept eating because the first bite was everything you were *told* it would be, so you expected each bite afterwards to be the same.

Do you see what happened? After that first bite, instead of trusting the person who gave you the chocolate, your faith was transferred from the person who gave you chocolate to the *chocolate itself*.

Your faith is in your expectation that every bite of chocolate you take will always taste like…well, chocolate!

Faith in God is a lot like eating chocolate. The first time you trusted God (put your faith in him), it was most likely because someone told you to.

Your parents or youth leaders or the preacher at your church told you it was the thing to do. They told you faith is a real thing. So since you know these people love you and want what's best for you, you believe them and 'do' it. You put your faith in God by asking him to do something for you.

I'm not talking about something selfish or 'out there'. I'm talking about something like helping you through a scary or tough situation. Or maybe something like giving you the courage to break a bad habit or resist the temptation to do something you know you shouldn't.

Or maybe you read about faith in your Bible and decided to take verses like Psalm 37:5-6 and Mark 11:22-24 out for a spin. And when you do, you find out it 'works'! God was there for you! You trusted him and he was there!

That's *real* faith. Once you realize God can be trusted and that he never breaks his promises, your faith is no longer in the person who told you to have faith, Now your faith is in God himself. Make sense?

Knowing faith is real doesn't always make it easy, though. Take Esther for example...

Esther was afraid to have faith. But thanks to Mordecai's encouragement, her faith saved the entire Israelite nation. (Esther 4:15-16).

Faith is what allowed Peter to step out of the boat onto the water and what allowed Paul to be bold for Christ no matter where he was, who he was with or what condition he was in.

You probably won't ever be royalty or find yourself trying out your water shoes. But having faith in God will put you where you need to be when you need to be there. And when your faith is your own, your life is going to be better than if you had an unlimited supply of chocolate to eat.

This doesn't mean life will be perfect. Faith isn't a guarantee against problems and painful experiences. But when you are faithful to God and have faith in him, you will see that nothing is bigger, better, or more important than your faith and relationship with God.

What About You

1. Why do we sometimes have a hard time putting our faith in God?

2. When and how has God rewarded you for having faith in him?

3. What do you think you can do to grow your faith?

4. Who do you admire because of their faith? Talk to them-ask them to pray for your faith to grow, too.

You've Gotta Push The Button

Have you ever been thirsty? I mean the kind of thirsty when your lips feel like they're glued shut because they are so dry?

I have and I can tell you it's not something you want to experience on a regular basis. It's not good for your body, either, so thankfully I didn't have to 'endure' having glued lips for too long.

That's the way it is for most of us, isn't it? The hard times usually don't last too long, but it sure doesn't feel good while they are going on, does it?

But can you imagine what it would be like to not be able to do anything to make your situation better?

Imagine being that thirsty with no water in sight. You would have a decision to make.

You could either stay there to shrivel up and die or you could gather every tiny bit of strength you have left to go looking for water. What would you do? Hopefully you start walking.

Imagine it. Progress is slow at first. You are ready to give up. But wait! What's that in the distance? Could it be? Yes, it's a vending machine and there are bottles of water inside! You may or may not try to pick up the pace, but either way you *finally* get there.

Now imagine yourself standing in front of the vending machine. Your hands are trembling as you slide your money in. Clink, clink, clink...clink (nothing's cheap these days).

Nothing happens. Nothing happens *and* you're still thirsty! Why? Because you're not done, that's why. If you have any hope of quenching your thirst, you've gotta push the button!!!

In other words, we have to become like the woman at the well in John 4. We need to know and believe in our heads and our hearts that Jesus is the 'water'...the *living water* that quenches the thirst for joy and contentment in our hearts and minds. We need to understand the words Jesus spoke in John 14:6...

Jesus answered, "I am the way and the truth and the life. No one comes to the Father except through me." ~John 14:6 NIV

Having a relationship with God is a lot like standing in front of a vending machine with your lips 'glued shut'. You may know *what* the Bible says about being a Christian, but not be living the life God expects you to live. You can *say* you want a relationship with God, but not do anything about it.

If you want to stop being thirsty, you've got to push the button. In other words, you have to give your whole life to God.

Have you heard of the Pharisees? The Pharisees were a group of Jewish people so caught up in obeying the laws God gave Moses and the Israelites that those laws became their God. The Pharisees are the people who would be standing in front of the vending machine without pushing the button. They refused to see Jesus for who he was (is) because he didn't look and act the way they thought he should. So instead, they did everything they could think of to make him look bad and they didn't stop until they had killed him.

Don't be a Pharisee. Don't go through life thirsty for God, but unable to quench your thirst because things aren't the way you think they should be. If you really want to *know* Jesus-to have the satisfaction and peace that comes from living the life he has in mind for you-then you've gotta push the button!

What About You

1. How thirsty are you to have a button-pushing relationship with God?

2. What keeps you from pushing the button? What parts of your life do you not want to give to God?

3. Do you think we have a hard time keeping God's expectations and guidelines (rules) from being more important than God? Why or why not?

Your Life Is An Occasion

In a scene from the movie, *Mr. Magorium's Wonder Emporium*, Mr. Magorium, the owner of the magical toy store, is spending the last day of his life with his best friend and store manager, a young lady named Molly Mahoney.

Naturally, Mahoney is sad to hear her friend is dying. Actually she goes into denial. She's not ready to say goodbye. But that's not her only problem.

Molly Mahoney is facing an inner struggle. She is trying to figure out if she will ever live up to her full potential *and* what that 'full potential' even is. So when Mr. Magorium tells her that he is going to die that very day and that he wants her to carry on the legacy of the toy store, she just doesn't know which way to turn.

Even worse, in her confusion she almost misses the life lesson Mr. Magorium wants to leave her with.

Mr. Magorium's final words to Molly are these: *"Your life is an occasion. Rise to it"*.

Wow! What a simple, yet profound statement. Mr. Magorium isn't the only one who has ever said something like that, though. His words of advice are a lot like the words in Proverbs...

"In his heart a man plans his course, but the Lord determines his steps."
~Proverbs 16:9 NIV

God, in all his wisdom, made each of us for a specific purpose. He gave each of us abilities and talents to use so that we can live up to our potential—just like Mr. Magorium told Molly to do.

What's more, he wants—even expects—us to do just that. But God doesn't want us to be like robots. He wants us to be our best self because WE want to. He wants us to love him because WE want to.

Right now you might be thinking you want to love God and you want to be your best, but like Molly, you aren't sure how. You aren't sure how to discover what your special purpose is. Am I right?

Well, here's some more good news. God doesn't expect us to figure things out on our own. He tells in Psalm 139:13-16 that he's had a plan for you…for me…for each of us-since the beginning of time. All we have to do is ask him what those plans are and he will tell us!

Wow! That's big…really big. But then, so is God.

Molly Mahoney stumbled and fumbled a bit, but in the end she came to understand that she didn't have to be famous or rich to reach her full potential. All she had to do was look inside her heart and do what she felt was good and true and right...for her. In other words, she just had to be HERSELF.

God wants to show you your self-who he created you to be. He wants you to rise to the occasion of your life-the life he has planned especially for you. Would you like that? Of course you would! So...what are you waiting for? Start rising!

What About You

1. Read each of the following: Jeremiah 29:11; Psalm 37:4; Proverbs 3:6; Joshua 1:8. What do you think each of these verses is saying?

2. What is your heart's desire? What is holding you back?

3. How can you honor God in following your heart's desire? Will you?

Being You Is Enough…No, Really It Is

In the movie, *Cool Runnings*, John Candy plays Irv Blitzer. Blitzer had been a double gold-medalist in the sport of bobsledding. But when it was discovered he had cheated, his medals were taken from him.

The opening scenes of the movie find him living in Jamaica; a lonely and bitter man trying to forget his former life.

His pity-party ends, however, when along comes some hopeful Olympians who have discovered who he is (but not what he has done). It takes a little time, a little smooth talking, and a lot of begging, but they finally convince him to be their coach; the coach of the first Jamaican Olympic bobsled team.

Sounds crazy, right? Most people in Jamaica have never even seen snow! That doesn't matter to these guys, though. They are determined and relentless in their efforts to succeed. And that is exactly what they do.

After relentlessly training and preparing, the team arrives in Vancouver, Canada to proudly represent their country. That would be stressful for anyone, but for these guys it was extra-hard. And to make matters worse, during the qualifying races a few days prior to the actual competition, the young Jamaicans became focused solely on winning a medal; so focused, in fact, that they begin imitating other athletes rather than being themselves.

The results are disastrous and almost cost them their spot in competition. Blitzer, in an effort to rebuild his team's confidence in their *own* abilities, confesses his past, i.e. losing his medals.

But he doesn't stop there. Blitzer also shares with him the important lesson he learned from the incident in hopes they will learn from his mistakes instead of making their own. This scene of the movie ends with him passing on to them a bit of wisdom we all need to understand and follow.

He says, "*A gold medal is a wonderful thing. But if you're not enough without it, you'll never be enough with it.*"

Take a minute to let that sink in. Read it again if you need to. Do you get it? Do you understand what Irv Blizter was saying? He was saying that while success and accomplishments and even *things* are nice to have, they cannot and will not bring you the happiness and contentment you are looking for. True happiness and contentment come from inside you.

Irv's advice is solid but it's not original. There are several instances in the Bible where we receive that same bit of wisdom. Paul, for instance, asked God to heal his eyes, but for some reason God chose not to. Instead, he told Paul…

"But he said to me, "My grace is sufficient for you, for my power is made perfect in weakness…." ~2nd Corinthians 12:9 NIV

So what's your 'gold medal'? What do you think you need to make your life all that and a bag of chips?

Whatever it is, I can tell you for sure and for certain…that's not it! And would you like to know *how* I know that?

The Bible. The Bible tells me that the only 'thing' that can make us feel complete and satisfied is to be completely sold-out for God.

There is no person, place, or thing that can do as much for you as God can. Being 'gold medal' material is a matter of a heart. Or should I say a joining of your heart to God's.

What About You

1. Where do you get your identity? The soccer field? The academic team? The cheerleading squad?

2. How would you feel if these things suddenly disappeared from your life?

3. God gives us our talents and passions, but what should you be doing to make sure these things don't become your god?

God Wants To Be The Cheese On Your Pizza

Let's talk about pizza. Crust-thick or thin. Sauce-traditional or Alfredo. Toppings-too many to list. And then you have the cheese. There are a lot of options when it comes to pizza-but cheese usually isn't one of them. Cheese is essential-it's just not pizza without cheese. And if it is to be considered a truly good pizza, the cheese must be unmistakably present in each and every bite.

Okay, so what does cheese on a pizza have to do with your relationship with God? I'm so glad you asked...

Abraham knew what it was to have God *cover* his whole life—to trust God for everything.

Abraham even trusted God to send that lamb so he wouldn't have to kill his son, Isaac.

Joseph trusted God with every part of his life-even when he served time in prison for a crime he didn't commit.

Mary faced the stares, gossip and ridicule of being an unwed pregnant teenage mom with grace and dignity because she didn't hold anything back from God. Her life was completely his.

Paul didn't hide or back down from anyone or anything because he knew God would work everything for good.

God was the cheese on their pizza (or whatever they ate back then). His love and wisdom covered everything they said and did.

God's love is something so intense and deeply rooted in every tiny particle of each and every one of us that we cannot even begin to comprehend it, BUT we can enjoy the benefits of it.

...so that Christ may dwell in your hearts through faith. And I pray that you, being rooted and established in love, may have power, together with all the Lord's holy people, to grasp how wide and long and high and deep is the love of Christ, and to know this love that surpasses knowledge—that you may be filled to the measure of all the fullness of God. ~Ephesians 3:17-19

God wants to be the cheese on your pizza, too. He doesn't want to be the crust that gets left on your plate because there's nothing on it. God won't settle for being a topping, either. Toppings are optional and God isn't optional-even though a lot of people think he is. No, God wants to be the cheese. He wants to be unmistakably present in each and every aspect of your life.

In fact, if you want to enjoy and experience the blessings God wants to give you, he won't settle for anything less than saturating your whole being; seeping into every inch of who you are...just like the cheese on your pizza.

How does that make you feel? Uncomfortable? Relieved? Thankful? Resentful? Safe? Smothered?

Don't worry if you don't think your answer is the 'right' one. What matters is that you live your life in such a way that someday soon the answer you give to that question will be 'saved by grace and lovin' it'.

What About You

1. What part or parts of your life have you not allowed God to seep into?

2. Why are you holding these things back from him?

3. What are some REAL actions you can take to make God the cheese on your pizza-life? Are you willing to start making these changes...today?

He's Not My Hero

Have you seen the movie, *October Sky*? *October Sky* is a movie based on the life of Homer Hickam and his friends; young men growing up in the 1960s in the coal mining town of Coalwood, W Virginia.

Most boys in Coalwood grew up resigned to the fact that they would follow in the footsteps of their fathers and grandfathers—footsteps that led straight into the coal mines, But Homer and his friends wanted more out of life than that.

Captivated by the launch of NASA's Sputnik, Homer and his friends entered a state science fair competition for high school students by building a rocket. But Sputnik wasn't Homer's only inspiration. One of the world's leading scientists at that time was German rocket engineer and scientist by the name of Werner Von Braun.

Homer read about Von Braun's accomplishments and admired his knowledge about rocketry science.

This all sounds really great, right? What's wrong with a guy wanting more out of life? Nothing, really, except for the fact that Homer's dad just couldn't wrap his head around it. He just didn't understand why Homer didn't want to be a miner. Or that's what it looks like, anyway.

I think Homer's dad was angry because he thought Homer's wanting more was his (Homer's) way of saying his dad wasn't someone he looked up to and admired.

Anyway...Homer was unaware of the fact that Von Braun was at the science fair...in the very same room as he was.

Von Braun even spoke to Homer, but because there was such a crowd of people and everyone was talking at once, Homer didn't even realize Von Braun was there.

The news reporters showed Von Braun at the science fair, though, so when Homer returned home, his dad sarcastically says to Homer, "I hear your hero, Werner Von Braun, spoke to you and you didn't even know it was him."

Homer, who wanted so desperately for his father to understand him replied, "Dad, I may not be the best, but I come to believe that I got it in me to be somebody in this world. And it's not because I'm so different from you either, it's because I'm the same. I mean, I can be just as hard-headed, and just as tough. I only hope I can be as good a man as you. Sure-Werner von Braun is a great scientist, but he isn't my hero."

Homer Hickam was just a teenager, but he had things in perspective. He understood that while it was certainly okay to look up to and admire people for their accomplishments and capabilities, they weren't hero material because he didn't really *know* them.

Who is your hero? Who do you want to be like?

Before you answer that question, take a few minutes to read the following scriptures.

Follow God's example, therefore, as dearly loved children and walk in the way of love, just as Christ loved us and gave himself up for us as a fragrant offering and sacrifice to God. ~Ephesians 5:1-2 NIV

Now ask yourself again…who is your hero? Who do you want to be like?

What About You

1. Who do you admire? Look up to? Aspire to be like? Why?

2. Have these people ever disappointed you or let you down? How did this make you feel?

3. Has God ever let you down? No, this isn't a trick question. There are times when we feel God isn't there for us. So...how did you feel? Do you still feel that way?

4. What do the verses you just read tell you about having a hero?

Stand Or Fall

Country singing star, Aaron Tippin, had a hit song a few years ago called *You've Got to Stand for Something*. The first two lines of the chorus of this song go like this…

*He'd say you've got to stand for something or you'll fall for anything
You've got to be your own man not a puppet on a string*

Hip-hop, rock, Christian, rap or country…it really doesn't matter what kind of music you listen to, you can't deny the truth of the words to this song. You've got to decide who you are and *whose* you are. You are either for or against (fill in the blank).

Trying to straddle the fence—being neutral or saying you have no opinion is in itself an opinion...the opinion of being a puppet on a string.

Jesus has a LOT to say about being a puppet on a string or a fence straddle, or whatever else you want to call it. In John 15 he says...

I am the vine; you are the branches. If you remain in me and I in you, you will bear much fruit; apart from me you can do nothing. If you do not remain in me, you are like a branch that is thrown away and withers; such branches are picked up, thrown into the fire and burned. ~John 15:5-6 NIV

In Romans 1:16, Paul tells us...

For I am not ashamed of the gospel, because it is the power of God that brings salvation to everyone who believes: first to the Jew, then to the Gentile. ~Romans 1:16 NIV

Do you live an unashamed life? Are you a branch that is firmly fixed to the vine? Are you thinking you can't answer both of these questions at once? That's okay. We'll take them one at a time.

An unashamed life. What's that look like? An unashamed life is one that is consistently Christ-like. There's not a different 'you' for church, your parents, your teachers and your friends. You talk the same, act the same, react the same and ARE the same wherever you go and whoever you spend time with. You aren't afraid to say 'no' to things and situations that go against what God expects from us.

Are you fixed to the vine? The vine, remember, is Jesus. Would anyone who spent more than a few minutes with you be surprised...even shocked...to hear you say you are a Christian?

What criteria do you use for making decisions about how to dress, who to date, where to hang out, what to do...?

If you can answer "No, they wouldn't be surprised" and if you use the Bible as your WWJD (what would Jesus do?) GPS, then it's pretty safe to say you are doing just fine. But remember: no matter where you are on this one, you can and should continually be growing.

When we prune (trim) a tree or a plant, we are sort of giving it a new look. We can even control how and where the new growth appears and which direction it goes.

That's what God wants—even expects us to let him do—when you say you are giving your life to him.

I know that's mind-boggling, but do you realize God's plan for *you* has been in place since the beginning of time?

Because of sin and the fact that he allows us to choose whether or not we obey, we have to be pruned and re-directed to live the life and be the person God created us to be.

The question is will you *let* yourself be pruned?

What About You

1. Would you say being a Christian is something you do or is it who you are?

2. Do your views on world issues (purity, homosexuality, greed, respect, etc.) match up with what God has to say?

3. If they don't, are you willing to be pruned? Is there anything you think you aren't willing to go through?

Are You Like The Hungry Caterpillar

Do you remember reading Eric Carle's *The Very Hungry Caterpillar* as a kid? It's a great book that tells the story of a baby caterpillar in search of something to eat.

If you'll remember, he doesn't have to look very long or hard to find a variety of things to munch on, does he? In fact, he has a virtual feast each and every day of the week.

There was just one problem—nothing he ate satisfied his hunger. Instead, it made him sick. Or as the book says, "...he had a stomach ache". Poor little caterpillar.

If you read the book you know it all works out okay, so let's take a minute to think about *why* the little caterpillar's hunger wasn't satisfied?

Was he not eating enough? Was he eating too much? Was he eating too fast? Too slow? No, no, no, and no.

The reason he was still hungry and dissatisfied in spite of all he had eaten was because he was eating the wrong stuff. Oranges, apples, and other fruits are fine for some animals, but not a caterpillar. Candy, cake, cheese, and meat are great for people, but not a caterpillar.

It wasn't until the caterpillar ate what he was supposed to eat (one little leaf) that he wasn't hungry anymore.

That's great, you say, but what's a kid's book got to do with being more like Jesus? A lot, actually.

I want you to stop and think about the things you fill *your* life with—friends, sports, clothes, cell phones, shoes, tablets, social media, money and all sorts of other stuff.

You believe you *have* to have these things; that you *have* to post, IM, or tweet everything that happens in a single day, and that you *have* to have that certain pair of jeans or everyone will look at you funny.

Am I right? But what happens when someone posts something about you that is untrue or hurtful?

What happens when that pair of jeans doesn't fit anymore or goes out of style? What happens when the phone you have is yesterday's news?

I know! I know! You go looking for the next best thing to satisfy the need/desire you have to feel good about yourself.

Well guess what—you're never going to get to that point. Not like that, anyway.

I've been there. I know how you feel. But I also know what you need to do to get to where you want and need to be. You've gotta 'eat a leaf'.

That's right—instead of filling yourself with a lot of stuff—to the point of having a physical, emotional, and spiritual stomach ache, you need to feast on the things God created that will leave you satisfied and fulfilled.

Do you want to know what those things are? Let's look…

For he satisfies the longing soul, and the hungry soul he fills with good things. ~Psalm 107:9

Delight yourself in the Lord, and he will give you the desires of your heart. ~Psalm 37:4
Keep your life free from love of money, and be content with what you have, for he has said, "I will never leave you nor forsake you." ~Hebrews 13:5

But seek first the kingdom of God and his righteousness, and all these things will be added to you. ~Matthew 6:33

And he said to them, "Take care, and be on your guard against all covetousness, for one's life does not consist in the abundance of his possessions." ~Luke 12:15

This doesn't mean it is wrong to have a cell phone, nice shoes, or to play sports—as long as you never put these things in front of your relationship with God, or think you have to have them in order to be happy. Do you understand the difference?

So...are you going to be a hungry caterpillar; thinking the newest, most popular, most expensive, or most exciting things are what life is all about? Or are you going to be a satisfied caterpillar who knows just where to go for real and lasting satisfaction?

What About You

1. What people or things do you think you need in life to make you happy?

2. How would you feel if you lost them all today?

3. How would losing them affect how you feel about God?

All He Really Wanted Was A Cup Of Sugar

Have you ever gossiped? Now before you answer let me ask you the same question a different way. Have you ever told someone something about another person that someone else told you?

Have you ever been the one to say something 'first' about someone or something you only *thought* was true (but didn't take the time to find out)?

Here's another question for you...have you ever been 'the someone' someone else was talking about?

That's a lot of 'something's and someone's', isn't it? But that's what gossip is—a lot of lip service about stuff that a) isn't true b) is meant to hurt someone or c) both.

That's what happened to Alexander P. Wolf. You probably know him as just the wolf who tried to eat the three little pigs. But in the book *The True Story of the Three Little Pigs* written by **Jon Scieszka** and **Lane Smith**, we learn the wolf wasn't as malicious as we are led to believe in the original version of the story.

According to Alexander P. Wolf, he went to each of the little pig's houses to borrow sugar to bake a cake. Honest (in his words).

If that's the way it really went down, we've been spreading rumors about a wolf for generations that aren't true!

I know you're probably thinking that's just a story and nobody cares. Maybe, but that kind of stuff happens all the time.

It happened to Joseph in the Bible. The book of Genesis tells the true story of how Joseph was falsely accused of raping his boss's wife and went to prison for it.

To be misunderstood or lied about is an awful experience. It's the kind of hurt that stays with you for years and years to come if not the rest of your life. You don't want to be responsible for causing someone that kind of pain do you?

There are six things the Lord hates, seven that are detestable to him: haughty eyes, a lying tongue, hands that shed innocent blood, a heart that devises wicked schemes, feet that are quick to rush into evil, a false witness who pours out lies and a person who stirs up conflict in the community. ~Proverbs 6:16-19 NIV

...to slander no one, to be peaceable and considerate, and always to be gentle toward everyone. ~Titus 3:2 NIV

But I tell you that everyone will have to give account on the day of judgment for every empty word they have spoken. ³⁷ For by your words you will be acquitted, and by your words you will be condemned.
~Matthew 12:36-37 NIV

What About You

1. Who have you talked about in a hurtful way? Ask God to forgive you and ask him for the strength to ask the person or people to forgive you, too. I know that can be a scary thing, but it's something you have to do. You can do it through a letter, a phone call, or in person as long as you do it.

2. What are some things you can do to make sure you don't participate in hurting people with gossip or rumors again?

3. Are you holding a grudge against someone who spread lies about you? Ask God to take away your anger and decide what you can and will do to show others these lies are not true.

Made You Look

WARNING: This chapter is mostly about or for girls. There's nothing in here boys *shouldn't* read, but there's not much in this chapter you guys will 'get'.

Cassie was practically screaming at her mom as they walked out of the store. Why? She was angry at her mom for not buying the clothes she'd picked out; a black belly-shirt that said 'hottie' in bright pink, shorts that were *really* short and a couple of other shirts that her mom thought were too old...for an eleven year-old.

Korynn openly admits she is proud of the fact that she wears clothes that will make the guys want to look at her body. "Hey," she says, "if you've got it you need to be proud of it. I want guys to want me." Korynn is fifteen.

All through high school Heather was known for wearing clothes to show off her curves. She was also a flirt, but drew the line at letting a guy go 'too far'.

But when she went away to college, a couple of guys decided her flirting was an invitation for more and didn't stop when Heather said 'no'. She was raped by both of them and is trying to get her education AND be a single mom. Heather is twenty.

I know you are under a lot of pressure to look a certain way, wear just the right clothes, have the right shoes and all the other things that go with this thing called 'image'.

I know the pressures of boy/girl relationships and of having sex or at least being sexy even at your age. I know these things because I've been where you're at right now and let me tell you, things haven't changed since then.

If you don't believe me, ask one of the eight girls in my graduating class who had babies our senior year and three of them who had ab baby our junior year. Or ask Julie, Lynn and Janell what it was like to have multiple (yes, multiple!) abortions in high school because they thought being sexually active was great, but their families weren't about to be embarrassed by their 'mistakes'.

These pressures have been around since almost the beginning of time.

- Leah married Jacob knowing he didn't love her, so she went to great lengths to make herself sexually appealing to him.

- Bathsheba was naked on the roof of her house; making you wonder if she really thought no one would see her.

- Esther had every kind of makeup, perfume and clothes at her disposal to make herself as pretty as possible for the king and was expected to use them.

- The woman at the well Jesus talked to was obviously sexually active outside of marriage.

- The woman Jesus saved from being stoned to death had been caught in bed with a man she wasn't married to.

- Paul writes in 1st Corinthians that a man has slept with his father's wife!

- Paul writes about sexual impurity and modesty in many of his other letters.

And finally, Jesus himself tells guys that looking at a girl lustfully (sexually) can send them to hell.

That's serious business, don't you think? But it's also something you girls have the power and responsibility to do something about. It's called dressing modestly.

Don't start rolling your eyes and mumbling about not looking like an old woman. That's not what I'm talking about. What I'm talking about is wearing clothes that don't give guys a reason to start thinking impure thoughts about you or girls in general when they see you. I'm talking about wearing clothes that don't give people the impression that you want people to think you are sexy. I'm talking about wearing clothes that say you honor God with your heart, mind and body.

But…but…what's that mean, you ask? It means:

- Not wearing tops or dresses that are low-cut or show cleavage.

- Not wearing t-shirts or sweatshirts with suggestive wording on them (hottie, sexy, luscious, available or crude, sexually explicit messages)

- Not wearing short-shorts or skirts/dresses (yes, the fingertip rule is a good one to follow)

- Not wearing pants or shorts that have ANYTHING written across the butt. Guys are visual. They can't help it. So when they look at what it says, they let the words fly right out of their mind and start thinking about your butt and then....

- Wearing clothing that fits too tightly.

- Wearing a bikini. A two-piece such as a tankini or a modest two-piece (think vintage) is fine.

You don't have to give up looking cute and stylish to be modest. You just have to be a little more selective in what you buy. But think about it like this…one day you are going to meet someone, fall in love and get married. Do you want him to be looking at girls/women wearing sexy, low-cut clothes that say "Take a look…I don't mind."? I didn't think so. You might also want to know that your future husband doesn't want other guys looking at you that way, either. So remember these three little words I always told my girls and still share with the girls in my youth group: MODEST IS HOTTEST.

Your beauty should not come from outward adornment, such as elaborate hairstyles and the wearing of gold jewelry or fine clothes. Rather, it should be that of your inner self, the unfading beauty of a gentle and quiet spirit, which is of great worth in God's sight. ~1st Peter 3:3-4 NIV

What About You

1. Go through your closet and take out everything that is see-through, low-cut, too tight and that has a sexual or suggestive message on it. Don't donate these items for others to wear. Instead, redo them to make them more modest.

2. Take a few minutes to ask your brother or a trusted guy-friend what he thinks about the way girls dress and how it hurts his relationship with God.

3. Commit to doing at least one thing every day to show others how beautiful you are from the inside out.

Whew! I'm Glad That's Over

Here is a science/biology question for you: what happens when you have a fever and it 'breaks' (your body returns to its normal temperature)?

I'm not going to give you the answer just yet, but we'll come back to it, I promise.

For now, though, I want you to think back to your recess and playground years. Do you remember trying to see who could hang from the monkey bars the longest?

You hung on for dear life even when your hands started to sweat and the sweat started running down your arm tickling you. Stupid sweat glands! Why did they have to go and mess things up!

Jesus knows exactly how you feel. He knows what it is to sweat and feel physical pain that's mixed up with emotional pain as well.

But Jesus knows something you don't. He knows that breaking into a sweat over what he was about to do wasn't a sign of weakness. He knows that it was actually a sign of great strength.

The night Jesus was arrested he went to the Garden of Gethsemane to pray. He went looking for his father, God, to fill him with peace and reassurance that what he was about to do was really necessary.

Hey, Jesus was a real person—just like you and me. He knew what was going to happen to him and he wasn't any too excited about it.

He'd seen plenty of guys hanging on crosses. He knew it was going to be unbearable from a human standpoint.

If you ask me, it was only natural for him to ask God if there was any other way.

Picture it. He was scared and nervous; more scared and nervous than you or I have ever been. Can you blame him? He was also about to do something you or I will never have to do. And in my opinion, the fact that he knew everything that was going to happen to him made it even scarier.

But instead of panicking, he started to pray. He prayed and he prayed...hard. Scripture tells us he prayed so hard he started to sweat; sweating so much that he sweat *actual drops of blood!* Talk about intense!

Intense doesn't even begin to describe it. But what most people don't know is that sweating drops of blood wasn't just a 'Jesus thing'. The act of sweating blood is a real condition or occurrence. It is called heamtidrosis.

Here's how it happens: when someone is under a tremendous amount of stress and anxiety, their blood vessels constrict (shrink); including the little net-like groups of blood vessels that surround our sweat glands.

When the anxiety passes, the blood vessels dilate grow back to normal size again. If this happens quickly, they grow or dilate really quickly and rupture or break. The blood inside the vessels then mixes with the sweat and the person literally sweats blood.

That's pretty amazing, isn't it? But do you know what is even *more* amazing? Go back and re-read the last paragraph; the one that explains hematidrosis. The whole blood/sweat thing doesn't happen until *after* the stress and anxiety are gone.

Do you know what this means? It means Jesus didn't sweat drops of blood because he was stressed over what he was going to have to do for us. He sweat blood because he was *relieved* to be at peace about dying and *ready* to make himself a human sacrifice for you and me. Call me crazy, but that takes intense to a whole new level! (Luke 22:39-44)

I know there are times when you get stressed. This world doesn't make life easy for us. But the good news is that when you get stressed you have Jesus to hold on to. So hold on and hold on tight. And when you start sweating, remember...sweat isn't a sign of weakness. It's a sign of strength and courage. It tells you that you know what you have to do and that you are ready to do it.

What About You

1. What is the most difficult thing you've ever had to do or face? How did you feel after the incident was over compared with how you felt at the beginning of the incident?

2. How does your relationship with Jesus affect how you handle stressful or scary situations? After reading this, what do you think you will do differently the next time you have a stressful situation to deal with?

3. What areas of your life do you need to let go of so that Jesus can give you the strength you need to handle them instead of trying to handle them yourself?

God Don't Make No Junk

According to studies done by doctors, counselors, statistics collectors, and teen magazines, the following are true statements about how you and your peers feel about yourselves:

- 80% of all teenage girls say they feel insecure when they see fashion models and movie stars in magazines on television or in a movie.

- After the age of 9, a girl's self-esteem begins to fall. For boys the age is 11.

- 90% of girls in junior high and high school are on a diet or have dieted.

- 25% of all boys in junior high and high school diet or closely watch what they eat.

- 6% of teenage boys *admit* to using unregulated steroids.

- 35% of teenage boys use supplements (vitamins and herbs/minerals) to increase muscle mass.

- Teenage girls are more afraid of being fat than they are of getting cancer, dying or nuclear war.

- Suicide is the third leading cause of death in teenagers and the reasons teenagers commit suicide all link back to poor self-esteem due to physical appearance, bullying and rejection.

- One out of every four girls has an eating disorder.

The list could go on and on but what's the point? It's obvious both boys and girls have a hard time with self-confidence.

Instead of being confident you are falling for the media's false and completely unrealistic ideas of what people should look like. Don't do that!

Wake up, ya'll! People don't look like the media says they do. They have lumps, zits, bumps, freckles, muffin tops, cellulite, and aren't nearly as buff as they want you to think they are. If you don't believe me, just search 'Photoshop errors' online and see what you come up with.

Think about it...if those people really looked like that, why would the media come down so hard on famous people when they look less than camera-ready?

But aside from all that, I want you to ask yourself this...why are you wasting so much time worrying about how you look?

God made you in HIS image (Genesis 1:26-27) which is not something you should take lightly. God + his image = you. That's nothing to be embarrassed or ashamed about. It's something to be proud of.

I know what you're thinking. You're thinking if we are all made in God's image, then why are some of us blonde and others red heads. Why are some people heavier than others? Why are some guys athletic while others can't catch a ball to save their life?

Not all animals look and act the same, but they were all made by God. Not every flower looks or smells the same, but they are all made by God. The earth is home to a variety of climates and landscapes, but they are all made by God. Get the point?

Now I don't take this as free pass to abuse your body with too much food, too much make-up, drugs, alcohol, tobacco or by starving/purging yourself, cutting or any other harmful activity. God made you the way you are because he knows it's just the way you need to be to do what he's designed you to do. And just in case you need me to remind you, God don't make no junk. God makes masterpieces and YOU are one of his masterpieces.

It's true—you are a masterpiece. You are created perfectly by the perfect creator. God knows this, now all *you* have to do is believe it!

For you created my inmost being; you knit me together in my mother's womb. I praise you because I am fearfully and wonderfully made; your works are wonderful, I know that full well. ~Psalm 139:13-14 NIV

What About You

1. How many of the statistics at the beginning of this chapter describe you?

2. What can you do to see yourself more like God sees you and less like the world thinks you should look? Suggestions: don't read secular fashion magazines, exercise and eat a healthy diet, dress modestly and get involved in serving in your church and your community.

3. Look at yourself in the mirror EVERY day and say, "I am God's masterpiece and God don't make no junk."

Wait Until You're Older

In the Disney™ movie, *Beauty and the Beast,* Lumiere, Cogsworth, Babette, Mrs. Potts and all the other objects/people in the castle looked on as Belle and the Beast spent a lovely evening together dining and dancing. As they watch, Cogsworth sings and Mrs. Potts echoes the phrase, *There may be something there that wasn't there before*….

Cogsworth, Mrs. Potts and the rest of the 'gang' know exactly what that 'something' is; love. But Chip, Mrs. Potts' teacup son, doesn't have a clue as to what's going on. So, being the normal kid he is (well, as normal as you can be and still be a teacup, anyway), Chip asks what's there that wasn't there before, to which his mother replies, "I'll tell you when you're older."

Has anyone ever said that to you? I'm going to take a guess and say yes. Like when you were four and asked your parents how babies get here, when you were six and asked how babies get here or when you were nine and asked why Uncle Larry and Aunt Shelly aren't married anymore. But your parents aren't the only ones that tell you to wait until you are older. These words come out of God's mouth, too.

Think about it...how many of you have asked yourself or someone else:

- *How* God got here

- How he can possibly hear everyone at the same time and know ever thing that has happened and will happen

- What happens when we die

- What heaven is like

The Bible (God's Word) doesn't go into much detail (if any) on these subjects. And do you want to know why? Because he knows we need to wait until we are older to be able to understand it all; 'older' being code for face to face with him in heaven. He knows that we simply aren't capable of comprehending what he's done and that if we knew these things we would not choose him out of love.

This frustrates a lot of people. I, on the other hand, say, "So what and who cares?" The Bible is filled with all sorts of assurances, promises, instructions, encouragements and jaw-dropping proof that God is the one true God and (if I allow him to be) his son, Jesus is my Lord and Savior. I don't care how God got here. I'm just glad he did.

I don't care how he was able to create all the unique and wonderful things in nature. I'm just glad he did.

I don't care what happens to our bodies when we die because he has promised that if I love and obey him it will be better than what I've got now and I trust him to keep his word.

I don' care what heaven is like because he says it will be wonderful and I believe he knows what he is talking about.

What about you? Don't you think your time would be better spent learning what God does tell us and developing a personal relationship with him based on that?

Don't you agree that God, the maker of the entire universe knows what he's talking about when he says we need to wait until we're older and shouldn't that be enough for us?

What About You

1. Spend some time in prayer thanking God for being so wise and for not giving you more than you can handle.

2. Read the book of James (New Testament). There's enough in there to keep you so busy you won't have time to think about those things that don't matter right now.

3. Take a walk in the woods, along a nature trail, on the beach…anywhere you can see God's amazing handiwork. Now think about it…if he can do all of that, surely he can handle everything else, too.

I Don't Need A Fleece, But Do You Have A...

Have you ever wished God would just tell you loud and clear what it is he wants you to do? Okay, dumb question—of course you have. Haven't we all? But have you ever asked God to give you a sign so you'd know *exactly* what you are supposed to do?

I have, and so have lots of other people; even people in the Bible. One in particular was Gideon...

Gideon was a member of the tribe of Manasseh—the smallest of the tribes of Israel. He was just an ordinary guy from an ordinary family to everyone around him.

But God saw past the ordinary. God saw the heart and mind of a great leader and warrior (a real-life superhero kind of guy).

God saw in Gideon just exactly who/what he needed to save the Israelites from the Midianites; a group of people who had been mistreating the Israelites for several years.

There was no doubt this was what God wanted Gideon to do. I say this because God himself talked to Gideon; giving him instructions as precise as any math equation you'll ever do.

Apparently Gideon didn't think that was enough. He wanted more. In the sixth chapter of Judges Gideon asks God for proof that he (God) said what Gideon thinks he heard him say.

Gideon tells God he's going to lay a fleece (a piece of wool) outside overnight. Gideon tells God that if he really is supposed to lead the Israelites into battle, the fleece will be wet with dew but the ground will be dry the next morning. It was.

But that *still* wasn't enough for Gideon. Next he apologetically asked God to give him more proof. This time Gideon asked God to make the ground wet and the fleece dry after being left out overnight again. It was, so Gideon led the Israelites into battle and won…just like God said they would.

There have been plenty of times over the years when I considered myself a Gideon; asking God for a sign or something tangible to prove he was working in my life. Most of the time I didn't get the signs I was asking for, but somehow things always worked out just fine—not necessarily the way *I* thought they would but always just they needed to. But I have to admit there were times I wondered about this; if God would do that for Gideon, why not for me?

I questioned if I were praying hard enough or if my motives were as right as I felt in my heart they were. I wondered what I was doing wrong.

One day I was praying; asking God why he wasn't answering my prayers like he did Gideon's. As soon as I finished saying those words, God answered my prayer by having these words play over and over in my head: "I already have. My Word is enough."

Could it really be that easy? Had all those signs I'd been praying for been right in front of me the whole time?

Yes! The answer is yes!

Gideon and a lot of others did not have the benefit of having the Bible to go anytime, anywhere when they need to hear God's wisdom, encouragement, teachings and his promises to never leave us and always do what is best for us.

Have you ever felt like Gideon; looking for a sign? Well, look no further because your sign is right here. It starts with Genesis and ends with Revelation. It's called the Bible and when it comes to knowing what God wants, it is all you need.

What About You

1. Ask God to tell you in your heart and mind what he wants for your life. Then listen. What do you hear? What thoughts run through your head and heart?

2. Start a prayer journal. Write down your prayer requests and the date you begin praying about these things. As you see the answers to these prayers in your life, write down when and how God answered each one.

3. Spend a few minutes thinking about Jesus' death on the cross. He died a horrible death as a punishment for something he'd not done. I can't think of a better sign. Can you?

The Bible Says...YOLO

I know you think you and your friends are the ones that made 'words' like yolo cool.

You also think you and your friends are the ones that discovered most of the latest fashion trends and that pop culture started with your generation.

Sorry to disappoint you, but you didn't do any of those things. If you don't believe me, well, just take a look in your attic or your grandma's attic and go through your parents' things from high school. *Then* you will know why people say everything old is new again.

As for the whole yolo thing, well, that's something that goes wayyyyyyyyyyy back; back before even Jesus was born.

What's even more interesting (weird is more like it)is the idea of you only live once so live it up while you can, comes from King Solomon.

Oh, and just in case you don't already know, other than Jesus, King Solomon is the wisest man who has ever lived or ever will live on earth. No, seriously, he really is. You can read it for yourself in 1st Kings, chapter three:

Solomon showed his love for the Lord by walking according to the instructions given him by his father David, except that he offered sacrifices and burned incense on the high places.

The king went to Gibeon to offer sacrifices, for that was the most important high place, and Solomon offered a thousand burnt offerings on that altar.

At Gibeon the Lord appeared to Solomon during the night in a dream, and God said, "Ask for whatever you want me to give you."

Solomon answered, "You have shown great kindness to your servant, my father David, because he was faithful to you and righteous and upright in heart. You have continued this great kindness to him and have given him a son to sit on his throne this very day."

"Now, Lord my God, you have made your servant king in place of my father David. But I am only a little child and do not know how to carry out my duties. Your servant is here among the people you have chosen, a great people, too numerous to count or number. So give your servant a discerning heart to govern your people and to distinguish between right and wrong. For who is able to govern this great people of yours?"

The Lord was pleased that Solomon had asked for this. So God said to him, "Since you have asked for this and not for long life or wealth for yourself, nor have asked for the death of your enemies but for discernment in administering justice, I will do what you have asked. I will give you a wise and discerning heart, so that there will never have been anyone like you, nor will there ever be. ~ 1st Kings 3:3-12 NIV

Before you get all excited; thinking that the guy God made smarter than anyone in the world is saying it's okay to have a yolo way of thinking, there's something else you need to read. It's something Solomon wrote in the book of Ecclesiastes.

Before you do that, though, I want to tell you about Corrie. Corrie is sixteen and has spent the last couple of years in psych wards, foster homes, juvenile detention centers, and in front of a judge swearing up and down she'll do better if she is allowed to return home.

Home is with her grandparents—grandparents who brought her home from the hospital when she was born because their daughter (Corrie's mom) was a seventeen year-old alcoholic who repeatedly ran away from home.

Corrie's grandparents have given parenting their best shot. They've raised her in the church, provided her with a safe, secure and loving environment.

Corrie would definitely argue against the 'loving' part of that statement; insisting that her grandparents have been too strict, controlling and over-protective.

While she might have a case 'against' them when it comes to being a bit strict, I think even you would have to agree that it's only natural for them to not want to repeat the same mistakes with Corrie that they felt they had made with her mom.

But anyway…Corrie knows right from wrong. She's a highly intelligent teenager who can easily achieve a 4.0 GPA when she's not getting into trouble. She knows what God expects of her (she was baptized when she was twelve) and she knows that the way she lives her life is not at all like a Christian should live. But if you ask her why, Corrie will tell you that she just doesn't care. She will tell you that she likes getting drunk but that it "…does make you do stupid things". She will tell you that she doesn't care what the Bible says about sex.

"I have a great body and I want to show it off. Guys like the way I 'do it'.

She will tell you that she believes in God but that she will not go to church because she likes the way she lives her life better than the way everyone at church tells you to live. She says she doesn't care where she ends up (heaven or hell). She just wants to have a good time getting there.

So what do you think? She sounds pretty tough, doesn't she? I know Corrie and I can tell you that she's not tough or bad or whatever term you want to use for someone who isn't afraid of anyone or anything.

Corrie is a lost, scared, sad, insecure little girl who is throwing her life away because she's too proud to admit she's in over her head and she's too selfish to give up the control she *thinks* she has over her life.

To put it bluntly, Corrie is throwing her soul to the devil for no other reason than she can.

Some of you probably read that thinking Corrie is one pathetic kid and that she needs someone to hit her with a great big dose of reality.

A few more of you probably think she deserves what she gets.

I bet there are even some of you who think Corrie is a victim—that she's never had what she really needs to heal from being rejected by her mom, not knowing who her dad is and all the baggage that goes with that.

You can think what you want, but the here's the cold, hard truth of the matter. Are you ready? According to the Bible, Corrie *does* deserve what she gets.

Read the following verse from Ecclesiastes. Read it carefully...then we'll talk.

You who are young, be happy while you are young, and let your heart give you joy in the days of your youth. Follow the ways of your heart and whatever your eyes see, but know that for all these things God will bring you into judgment. ~Ecclesiastes 11:9 NIV

Did you see it? It's right there in black and white. The Bible...the *Bible* says it is okay to do whatever you want to do. But it doesn't stop there, does it? This verse very clearly says that we can do whatever we want, but that in the end we will have to answer to God for the choices we make. In other words, you play...you pay.

God created us. He knows we aren't perfect and that we are going to sin. He knows we aren't always going to make the best choices...or the Godliest ones, either.

But he also knows our hearts. He knows whether or not we make poor choices because we want to or don't care about our relationship with him or if these choices are temporary lapses in judgment, caving to peer pressure once in a while or just plain old immaturity that you will outgrow as you grow in your relationship with God.

So what do you think? What does the verse in Ecclesiastes do to change how you make decisions? Or does it?

What About You

1. When have you decided to do something even when you know it's wrong?

2. How did you feel afterwards?

3. Now that you know what the Bible says about living with the choices you make, will it change what you do? Who your friends are? How you interact with your boyfriend or girlfriend? Where you go?

What Kind Of House Do You Live In

"Gloves are houses for hands. Toasters are houses for bread. Fences are houses for land and hats are houses for heads. Cups are houses for water or tea and sometimes dogs are houses for fleas."

I could go on and on and on...just like one of my favorite story books, *A House is a House for Me*. Not only is the book creative, fun and quirky, it's philosophical without even trying to be. It makes you realize that everything is a house for something.

The question, I want to ask you, though, is: What kind of house do you live in?

I'm not talking about a little house in a quiet neighborhood or a house big enough you never have to see your family if you don't want to.

I'm not talking about an apartment in a part of town no one wants to go to unless they have to or a house in the country with a big yard to play in.

I'm talking about the house *you* live in—the you that feels happy or sad. The you that knows what you what to do with your life or the you that wants to be five years old again so you don't have to make that decision. The you that is convinced your parents don't understand you, but wants them to fix things when they go wrong. The you that can't imagine your life without swimming or basketball or drama club. The you that loves country music but can't stand the smell of vinegar. The you that doesn't understand how anyone can abuse a child or con old people out of their life savings. The you…that makes you, you! What does that you live in?

God created you; giving you a 'house' that is fearfully and wonderfully made. He made it uniquely yours and what's really cool is that he knew from the very beginning (back in the "In the beginning…." days) just exactly what he wanted each of us to look like and be.

For you created my inmost being; you knit me together in my mother's womb. I praise you because I am fearfully and wonderfully made; your works are wonderful, I know that full well. My frame was not hidden from you when I was made in the secret place, when I was woven together in the depths of the earth. Your eyes saw my unformed body; all the days ordained for me were written in your book before one of them came to be. ~Psalm 139:13-16 NIV

God went to a lot of trouble to make sure your thoughts, feelings, emotions, passions and heart's desires live in a custom-made house; a house no one else could be comfortable or happy in. What's more, because he's the one who created you and designed your house, he knows better than anyone what is best for you.

Have you ever thought about it like that?

Who do you go to when you have a cavity? It's not nice lady at the bank, is it? Of course not! You trust your teeth to the dentist because the dentist is the only one qualified to care for your teeth. So what possible reason could you possibly have for trusting anyone but God (the one who created you) with your house…your life?

Being a Christian isn't something you do. It's who you are.

You can't do Christianity when it's easy or looks good. You can't just say you are a Christian and it be true, no more than saying you are the President of the United States makes you the President.

So let me ask you: Do you treat your house with respect; feeding it healthy food and getting plenty of rest and exercise? Do you value your body's sexuality and are you saving yourself for your future spouse? Do you use the talents God created within you to serve him? Do you make decisions God calls good? Do you dress modestly? Would you be okay with Jesus hanging out with you as you go about your day?

I sure hope you can answer 'yes' to these questions, because your 'house' (body) is meant to be God's home and he is more than ready to move in and make himself comfortable.

What About You

1. If Jesus cam to spend a few days with you, what would he have to say about the way you dress? The way you talk? The things you do? The places you go?

2. What can you do to make your body a better home for God?

3. If you have accepted Jesus as your Savior, how does it make you feel to know the Holy Spirit is living in you?

4. If you haven't accepted Jesus as your Savior, how different do you think your life would be if you did?

Sometimes You Do...Sometimes You Don't...But It Always Works Out Just Fine

Can you smell it? You know...the smell of new crayons, glue sticks, new tennis shoes, and unsharpened pencils. It's time to buy new school supplies!

There's something exciting about starting a new school year, isn't there? There's something about getting new school supplies that makes you feel hopeful.

You hope you get a certain teacher and that your best friends are in some or most of your classes.

Sometimes you get the teacher you want...and sometimes you don't. Sometimes your friends are in your classes. Sometimes they aren't.

You always hope your school ID picture doesn't look like a mug shot. Sometimes it does...sometimes it doesn't.

You hope you get a certain lunch hour. Sometimes you do...sometimes you don't.

With each new school year comes a little excitement and yes, even a few disappointments. But then life is like that, isn't it?

So remember: it's really not the end of the world if you don't always get the teacher you want. You're still going to learn what you need to learn to move up to the next grade.

And the world really won't stop turning if you aren't in the same homeroom or lunch period as your best friend—I promise.

The ID pictures? Sorry, no guarantee on that one, either. I mean is there anyone who can take a good picture when you have all of ten seconds to step into place and say 'cheese' before the weird guy behind the camera takes one shot and hollers "Next!"?

All of these things are okay because they help you become more resilient. That means they make you stronger. They teach you that you can't always have things your way. They help you learn to compromise and take turns. They also teach you that you can't always control your surroundings. But most important of all, these situations can teach you to have faith in God that no matter what happens, when you trust him to take care of you, he will always do what's best for you.

So whenever it's time to start a new school year, don't worry if you have to choose a $15 dollar back pack instead of a $50 one.

Don't whine and moan because you have first lunch period instead of third like 'everyone' else does. Just go with it and trust God to help you make the best of it.

For I know the plans I have for you," declares the Lord, "plans to prosper you and not to harm you, plans to give you hope and a future. ~Jeremiahs 29:11 NIV

What About You

1. What do you usually do when things don't go the way?

2. When has something good happened even when things didn't go the way you wanted them to?

3. Do you have a hard time trusting that Jesus will always do what is best for you? Why or why not?

Don't Be Afraid To Look Under A Few Rocks...
Just Be Careful When You Do

Olivia and her mom spent two days gathering and hauling big rocks for a landscaping project at their house. These weren't just any rocks, though. They were rocks from the house Olivia's great-great-great grandparents used to live in. Yah, that's three greats, which means those rocks were really, really old—like every other rock.

Anyway, while she and her mom climbed around on what remained of the 'old home place' deciding which rocks to take (that's code for which ones they could lift into the back of the truck), they laughed about how crazy they were to be 'risking their lives' for a bunch of old rocks. But that didn't stop them. They were actually having too much fun.

Every time Olivia started to pick up a rock, though, her mom warned her to be careful...very, very careful because of the possible dangers hiding under the rocks (that's code for snake).

FYI: Olivia and her mom reported they were *very* thankful to say that in all the rocks they picked up they never saw one snake. Nada. Zilch. Zero. None.

Olivia said, "Even if we had seen a snake I can say with complete certainty that after we had quit screaming and doing that little "I just saw a snake" dance, we would have been right back at it."

`Why? Because they wanted the rocks. They weren't about to let the fact that something may or may not be hiding under one of those rocks keep them from getting the job done.

What about you? Are you willing to look under a few rocks in life to find what you want? Are you are confident enough in who you are to look under the rocks called **trying something new, speaking up for what is right, and being confident enough in their abilities and personality** to follow their dreams?

Looking under a few rocks is something we all have to do if we really want to live up to our potential. Just be sure when you find things like **peer pressure, danger,** and **sin,** that you run away as fast and as far as you can.

What About You

1. What is the scariest thing you've ever done? Why was it scary?

2. What do you say to someone when they want you to do something you know you shouldn't?

3. Do you believe Jesus will help you use your talents to be the best person you can be? Why or why not?

Made in the USA
Columbia, SC
06 May 2018